LIGHTNING BOLT BOOKS™

How Do Trains Work?

Buffy Silverman

Lerner Publications • Minneapolis

Lerner Publications Company
A division of Lerner Publishing Group, Inc.
241 First Avenue North
Minneapolis, MN 55401 USA

For reading levels and more information, look up this title at www.lernerbooks.com.

Library of Congress Cataloging-in-Publication Data

Silverman, Buffy, author.
    How do trains work? / Buffy Silverman.
      pages cm. — (Lightning bolt books. How vehicles work)
    Summary: "Young readers will love this exciting, in-depth yet accessible look at trains, including how they work, the special equipment they need, and how they tote thousands of tons of cargo down the tracks"—Provided by publisher.
    Includes bibliographical references and index.
    Audience: 5–8
    Audience: K–3
    ISBN 978-1-4677-9500-5 (lb : alk. paper) — ISBN 978-1-4677-9687-3 (pb : alk. paper) — ISBN 978-1-4677-9688-0 (eb pdf)
    1. Railroad trains—Juvenile literature. I. Title
TF148.S48 2015
625.2—dc23   2015014864

Manufactured in the United States of America
2-42817-20613-8/11/2016

Table of Contents

Here Comes the Train!

Wooo, wooo! A horn blows as a train nears a road. A bell rings. A gate with flashing lights lowers across the road.

Cars stop when a train rumbles past.

4

A sensor is on the tracks near the road. The train's steel wheels connect to each other with a steel bar. When the train's wheels pass over the sensor, they complete a circuit.

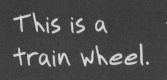

This is a train wheel.

Electricity flows through the circuit. It sends a signal to lower the crossing gate. The signal turns on the flashing lights and bells.

These flashing lights tell drivers a train is coming.

This long train has one hundred cars. Hooks between each car join them together. The train weighs 12 million pounds (5.4 million kilograms). That is heavier than twelve jumbo jets!

Powerful Locomotives

A locomotive pulls the train along the tracks. The locomotive needs a lot of power to move the heavy train.

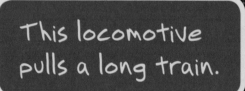

This locomotive pulls a long train.

The **locomotive** has a powerful diesel engine. The huge engine changes diesel fuel into energy that moves the train.

Pistons move inside the engine. The pistons connect to a drive shaft. It turns and powers a generator. The generator makes electricity.

This is a piston for a train's engine.

A worker checks a train's motors.

Electricity is sent to four motors under the locomotive. Each motor turns a small gear.

The small gear turns a large gear. The large gear is on an axle. The axle turns the locomotive's wheels.

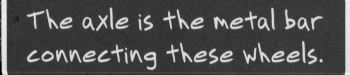

The axle is the metal bar connecting these wheels.

The engineer rides in the cab at the front of the locomotive. The engineer drives the train.

A worker changes one of the train's brake pads. The Pads push against the wheels. The pads slow the wheels, and the train stops.

Do you see the brake pad?

The four motors under the locomotive can also slow the train. They make a lot of heat. Giant fans suck the heat away from the motors and out through the top of the locomotive.

Tracks

Train wheels run along two steel tracks. Railroad ties connect the tracks.

Most railroad ties are made of wood.

When a car travels on a highway, its tires rub against the road. This rubbing is called friction. Engines must work harder to move against friction.

Do you see where these train wheels touch the track?

Trains make very little friction. Only a tiny part of a train wheel rubs against a track. It takes little energy to pull heavy trains because there is little friction.

The engineer does not steer the train. The train follows the tracks. Some tracks go straight. Some curve. These tracks tunnel through a mountain.

Trains switch to different tracks to go in new directions.

Many train tracks come together in a city. Switches move trains from one track to another. They let trains safely pass one another.

Freight Trains

Long freight trains crisscross the country. They carry coal and corn. They move wood and oil.

This train car is being loaded with coal.

Hopper cars are open at the top. The car can be loaded and unloaded quickly.

A tank car carries liquid. Liquid is loaded through a hatch on top of the car. Some tank cars carry corn oil. Other tank cars haul chemicals or fuel.

These tank cars will be filled with liquid.

Passenger Trains

Passenger trains move people from place to place. People board a train at a train station.

Many people travel on high-speed trains. The trains' smooth shape lets them slip through the air and zoom on the tracks.

Special tracks are built for high-speed trains. Only high-speed trains use the tracks. The tracks go as straight as possible so high-speed trains can zoom!

This subway train has arrived at the station!

Some cities have train systems for people called subways. Subways zip through tunnels below city streets. All trains have one thing in common. They get people and things where they need to go!

Diagram

horn

cab

locomotive

cars

5698

5698

wheels

tracks

Train

Fun Facts

- Locomotives are heavy! Some locomotives weigh more than 400,000 pounds (181,437 kg). Their huge engines can do the work of up to six thousand horses.

- Some trains do not have locomotives. Each car has its own power. Some trains have a generator for each car. Other train cars run on electricity from an overhead wire or a third rail.

- Someday you might ride on a train with no wheels. Powerful magnets let a maglev train float above the track. Since the train doesn't rub against the track, there is no friction. The train zooms!

Glossary

circuit: the complete path of an electric current

diesel: a type of fuel and an engine powered by this fuel

engine: a machine that gives a train power to move

engineer: a person who drives a train

generator: a machine that makes electricity

locomotive: the vehicle at the front of a train that pulls the train cars

piston: a part of an engine that moves up and down and makes other parts move

sensor: a piece of equipment that responds to motion

Further Reading

All about Trains: History and Latest Trends
http://easyscienceforkids.com/all-about-trains

Floca, Brian. *Locomotive.* New York: Atheneum Books for Young Readers, 2013.

National Geographic Channel: Assembling the Subway Car
http://channel.nationalgeographic.com/ultimate-factories/videos/assembling-the-subway-car

Spotlight: Trains
http://www.kidsdiscover.com/spotlight/trains-for-kids

Train Facts for Kids
http://www.sciencekids.co.nz/sciencefacts/vehicles/trains.html

Wetterer, Margaret K. *The Midnight Adventure of Kate Shelley, Train Rescuer.* Minneapolis: Graphic Universe, 2011.

Index

Photo Acknowledgments

The images in this book are used with the permission of: © iStockphoto.com/ RiverNorthPhotography, p. 2; © Mike Danneman/Moment/Getty Images, p. 4; © CrackerClips Stock Media/Alamy, p. 5; © Paskee/Dreamstime.com, p. 6; © Radharc Images/Alamy, p. 7; © Paul Matthew Photography/Shutterstock.com, p. 8; © Lightpainter/Dreamstime.com, p. 9; © 17s/Dreamstime.com, p. 10; © Agencja Fotograficzna Caro/Alamy, p. 11; © Hupeng/Dreamstime.com, p. 12; © CTK/Alamy, p. 13; © European Press Agency/Alamy, p. 14; © Olever Perez/Dreamstime.com, p. 15; © Haydn Adams/Dreamstime.com, p. 16; © iStockphoto.com/DaveAlan, p. 17; © soleg/ Deposit Photos, p. 18; © Jim Parkin/Alamy, p. 19; © iStockphoto.com/zennie, p. 20; © Ketian Chen/Dreamstime.com, p. 21; © Cultura Creative/Alamy, p. 22; AP Photo/Larry MacDougal, p. 23; © Bruce Bisping/Minneapolis Star Tribune/ZUMA Press, p. 24; © iStockphoto.com/ollo, p. 25; © ortodoxfoto/Deposit Photos, p. 26; © rorem/Deposit Photos, p. 27; © Laura Westlund/Independent Picture Service, p. 28; © Joop Kleuskens/ Dreamstime.com, p. 30.Front cover: © Dan Van Den Broeke/Dreamstime.com.

Front cover: © Dan Van Den Broeke/Dreamstime.com.

Main body text set in Johann Light 30/36.